REAL LIFE SEA MONSTERS

Moray Eels

by Ruth Owen

PowerKiDS press™

New York

Published in 2014 by The Rosen Publishing Group, Inc.
29 East 21st Street, New York, NY 10010

Produced for Rosen by Ruby Tuesday Books Ltd
Editor for Ruby Tuesday Books Ltd: Mark J. Sachner
US Editor: Joshua Shadowens
Designer: Emma Randall

Photo Credits:
Cover, 1, 4–5, 6–7, 8–9, 10–11, 12–13, 14, 16–17, 19, 20–21, 22–23, 24–25,
26–27, 29 © Shutterstock; 15 © Zina Deretsky; 18 © Barb Makohin.

Library of Congress Cataloging-in-Publication Data

Owen, Ruth 1967–
 Moray eels / by Ruth Owen.
     pages cm. — (Real life sea monsters)
 Includes index.
 ISBN 978-1-4777-6253-0 (library) — ISBN 978-1-4777-6254-7 (pbk.) —
 ISBN 978-1-4777-6255-4 (6-pack)
 1. Morays—Juvenile literature. I. Title.
 QL638.M875O94 2014
 597'.43—dc23

                              2013026401

Manufactured in the United States of America

CPSIA Compliance Information: Batch #W14PK7: For Further Information contact: Rosen Publishing, New York, New York at 1-800-237-9932

CONTENTS

MEETING A MONSTER

You're having an amazing underwater adventure, scuba diving on a coral reef.

You photograph the beautiful coral and marvel at the rainbow-colored **fish**. Then, suddenly, you notice a small dark **crevice** between some rocks. As you peer into the gloom, you wonder, what lives in here?

You get your answer fast, as a terrifying, snake-like head emerges from the darkness. Suddenly, you're face to face with a mouthful of vicious teeth. The creature looks like something from a monster movie, but this sea monster is real.

You've just disturbed a moray eel, and that menacing mouthful of sharp teeth is powerful enough to tear through your wet suit and snap off your fingers like twigs!

Moray eels may look a little like snakes, but they are actually fish.

A fangtooth moray eel

WHAT IS A MORAY EEL?

Looking like snakes, but belonging to the fish family, moray eels are fierce, underwater hunters.

Some **species**, or types, of moray eels are just a few inches (cm) long. Others grow to be twice the length of an adult human!

These **predatory** fish live in warm oceans all over the world. Some live on the seabed, burrowing into the sand. Others hide in cracks between rocks or in crevices on coral reefs.

The way that moray eels move through the water also seems snake-like. As these fish swim, they move their whole bodies from side to side in an S-shaped curve.

A moray eel swimming

Most fish can only swim forward. Moray eels can swim forward and backward.

Giant moray eel

Crevice in coral reef

PHYSICAL FACTS

Unlike other fish, moray eels do not have scaly skin. Their smooth skin is covered with a layer of slimy mucus.

The mucus on an eel's skin allows it to slither through cracks in rocks and coral reefs without getting scratched.

Fish usually have several fins on their bodies, including a dorsal fin on their backs and pectoral fins on either side, as does the clown fish below. Moray eels do not have pectoral fins. They do have an extra-long dorsal fin that runs from behind their head all the way along their back.

Moray eels cannot see very well. Their eyes are often tiny compared to the size of their heads.

Dorsal fin

Clown fish

Pectoral fins

Moray eel

Dorsal fin

Dorsal fin

Moray eel

A moray eel's dorsal fin has very thick skin to keep it from getting cut or scratched as the eel moves through small, rocky spaces.

OPEN WIDE

Moray eels look threatening because their mouths are usually open.

Most of the time, however, a moray eel isn't about to bite something. The eel has its mouth open to help it breathe.

In order to get the **oxygen** they need to live, fish use **organs** called **gills**. A fish takes in water through its mouth and passes it out through its gills. As water passes through the gills, these organs remove oxygen from the water and pass it into the fish's blood.

In order to get enough water moving through its gills, a moray eel continually opens and closes its mouth.

Gills

A moray eel's small, circular gills can be seen on the side of its body.

THE HUNT

By day, a moray eel rests in its lair. It might stay completely hidden, or wait with just its head showing.

At night, the creature emerges from its hiding place to hunt. The eel swims over the reef, moving in and out of cracks searching for **prey**.

Sometimes, a moray hunts by **ambushing** its meal. It waits in a crevice in a rock. As an unsuspecting creature passes by, the eel grabs the animal in its fearsome jaws.

Eels eat many different types of ocean animals. They hunt for fish and octopuses, and some types even eat hard-shelled **crustaceans**, such as crabs and lobsters.

Moray eels use their excellent sense of smell to find prey.

JAWS

A creature trapped in the mouth of a moray eel is doomed.

The sharp teeth in the eel's mouth grab and hold the animal. Then, something truly horrifying happens.

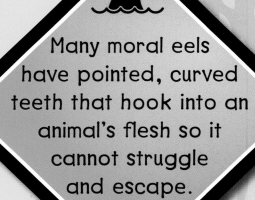

From deep inside the eel's throat, a second set of sharp, curved teeth spring forward to grab the prey! These teeth drag the eel's victim into its esophagus, which is the long tube that connects the eel's mouth to its stomach.

Some other types of fish also have a second set of jaws. Usually, however, these much smaller teeth don't move and are only used for grinding food. A moray eel's second set of jaws, however, can move, spear its prey, and drag a creature to its death!

Many moral eels have pointed, curved teeth that hook into an animal's flesh so it cannot struggle and escape.

Moray eel

Jaw

Second set of jaws

Second jaws
move forward

CLEAN-UP CREW

Most creatures don't want to get close to a moray eel's terrifying, toothy grin. For some, however, it's how they make their living.

A visit into a moray eel's mouth is like an "all you can eat" buffet for a cleaner shrimp. These tiny creatures work in partnership with eels. The shrimp gets to snack on leftovers trapped between the eel's teeth. For the eel, a visit from the shrimp is like flossing, and keeps the larger animal's mouth clean and healthy.

Shrimp aren't the only members of the eel's clean-up crew. Small fish called cleaner wrasse regularly get to work at keeping an eel's skin clean and healthy. The wrasse eat pieces of dead skin and tiny **parasites** that live on the eel.

Cleaner wrasse

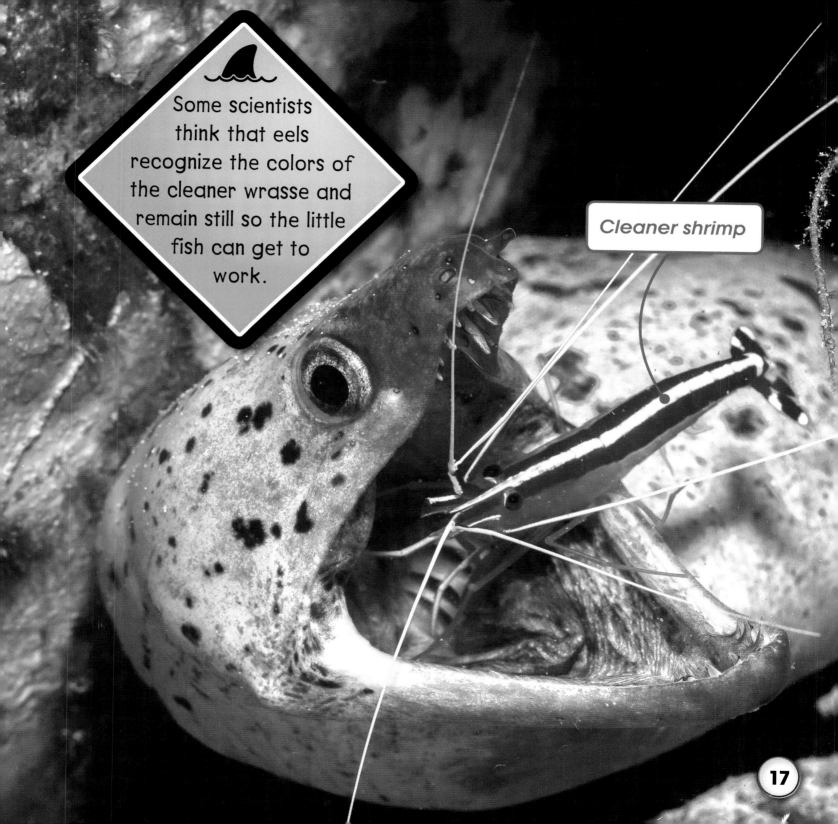

Some scientists think that eels recognize the colors of the cleaner wrasse and remain still so the little fish can get to work.

Cleaner shrimp

MINI MORAYS

When two moray eels are ready to **mate**, the animals spend some time with their mouths wide open gaping at each other.

Then, in a dance-like movement, they wrap their long bodies around each other. As the eels mate, the female's eggs are released into the water.

Tiny, young eels called **larvae** hatch from the eggs. These eel larvae look like leaf-shaped ribbons. Their bodies are completely see-through.

The larvae float in the ocean for about eight months until they change into little eels called elvers. The elvers swim to a coral reef or rocky, underwater place to begin their lives as hunters. In time, the mini morays grow into their fanged, fearsome adult selves.

Moray eel larva

A pair of moray eels

Female moray eels do not take care of their eggs or young.

MEET SOME MORAYS

There are 200 different species of moray eels living in the world's oceans.

The green moray eel is one of the most common types. This eel's skin is actually blue, but the mucus covering its body is yellow. The combined colors of the eel's skin and mucus give the animal its greenish color.

Blue ribbon eels have fluttery, leaf-like parts on their nostrils. One theory is that these parts developed to look a little like fish. These fake fish attract other fish to come close to the eel's jaws.

Green moray eel

Blue ribbon eel

Fluttery nostrils

The little white-eyed moray eel grows to about 16 inches (40 cm) long.

White-eyed moray eel

MORAY MONSTERS

The two most terrifying moral eels are probably the fangtooth and the giant moray eel.

A fangtooth moray eel has very long jaws. Its mouth is crammed with sharp teeth that look as if they are made of glass.

The giant moray eel is not the longest member of the moray eel family, but by weight it is the largest. Giant morays have dark skin with leopard skin-type spots. These giants grow to nearly 10 feet (3 m) long, and an adult can weigh up to 66 pounds (30 kg).

Giant moray eels feed on fish, octopuses and squid, and crustaceans. They also hunt and eat other eels.

The longest moray eel is the slender giant moray eel. Slender giants grow to 13 feet (4 m) long.

A giant moray eel

Fangtooth moray eel

23

A TEAM PLAYER

Giant moray eels are happy to hunt as part of a team if the prize is right.

Coral groupers are fast-swimming fish that can easily catch prey in open water. If a grouper's prey hides among rocks or coral, though, the large fish can't follow.

When this happens, a grouper will sometimes swim to a giant moray and shimmy its body. This shimmy is a signal to tell the moray to join the hunt. Sometimes, the grouper shows the moray exactly where to look by performing a headstand over the place where prey is hiding.

The giant moray squeezes between the rocks or coral and flushes out the animals from their hiding place. This amazing teamwork allows both the grouper and the moray to eat.

While many animals hunt as a team, it's unusual for two animals from different species to team up!

A giant moray eel searching for prey

A coral grouper

WATCH YOUR FINGERS

Many scuba divers who visit coral reefs are hoping to see a moray eel.

Sometimes, divers are even tempted to carry food to attract these wild animals to come to them. The morays smell the food and come close. Unfortunately, morays can't tell the difference between a tasty morsel of food and a diver's fingers. Many divers have had their fingers bitten off by moray eels!

Sometimes, divers put their hands into cracks between rocks. This is a very foolish thing to do, as the crack could be a moray's hiding place. When a moray feels it is in danger, it will do what comes naturally and bite!

Moray eels don't deliberately attack people. They might, however, seriously hurt a person by accident.

CRUNCH!

In 2005, scuba diver Matt Butcher and a team of other divers were watching a giant moray eel in the ocean off Thailand.

Nicknamed Emma, the giant moray was used to divers visiting and feeding her.

On that day, as Matt tried to get some sausages out of a plastic bag, the hungry eel suddenly clamped her jaws onto his hand. Matt tried to get free, but then there was a terrible, crunch-click noise. Emma had bitten off Matt's thumb and swallowed it!

With blood gushing from his hand, Matt made it back to his boat and to a hospital. Matt survived the accident and, in time, had one of his toes attached to his hand to create a new thumb.

Matt doesn't blame Emma the moray eel for eating his thumb. He knows she was only doing what comes naturally!

GLOSSARY

ambushing (AM-bush-ing)
Attacking from a hidden position.

coral reef (KOR-ul REEF)
Underwater masses of hard, rocklike matter made from the skeletons of tiny sea animals, called corals, that are joined together. When a coral dies, its skeleton remains, so the mass of coral grows larger and larger.

crevice (KRE-vus)
A crack or gap in rock or another hard material.

crustaceans (krus-TAY-shunz)
Animals with hard shells instead of skeletons. Crabs, lobsters, and shrimp are all crustaceans.

fish (FISH)
Cold-blooded animals that live in water. Fish breathe through gills and have a skeleton. Most fish lay eggs.

gills (GILZ)
Body parts that an underwater animal uses for breathing. The gills take oxygen out of water and send it into the animal's body.

larvae (LAR-vee)
The young of some animals, including fish and insects.

mate (MAYT)
To get together to produce young.

mucus (MYOO-kus)
A thick, slimy liquid that a body part produces, usually as a form of protection.

organs (OR-gunz)
Body parts such as the brain, heart, lungs, or gills.

oxygen (OK-sih-jen)
The gas in air that humans and other animals need to breathe.

parasites (PER-uh-syts) Organisms (living things) that live on and get their food from another living thing.

predatory (PREH-duh-tor-ee)
Living by hunting and eating other animals.

prey (PRAY)
An animal that is hunted by another animal as food.

scaly (SKAY-lee)
Having skin covered with scales. Scales are small segments of overlapping skin. Fish and reptiles, such as snakes, have scaly skin.

species (SPEE-sheez)
One type of living thing. The members of a species look alike and can produce young together.

WEBSITES

Due to the changing nature of Internet links, PowerKids Press has developed an online list of websites related to the subject of this book. This site is updated regularly. Please use this link to access the list:

www.powerkidslinks.com/rlsm/moray/

READ MORE

Miller, Tori. *Eels*. Freaky Fish. New York: PowerKids Press, 2009.

Niver, Heather Moore. *20 Fun Facts About Moray Eels*. Fun Fact File: Fierce Fish! New York: Gareth Stevens Learning Library, 2012.

Rand, Casey. *Giant Morays and Other Extraordinary Eels*. Creatures of the Deep. Mankato, MN: Capstone Press, 2012.

INDEX